BILLY JOEL

GLASS HOUSES

Additional editing and transcription by David Rosenthal

ISBN 978-1-5400-6738-8

HAL•LEONARD®

Visit Hal Leonard Online at
www.halleonard.com

Contact us:
Hal Leonard
7777 West Bluemound Road
Milwaukee, WI 53213
Email: info@halleonard.com

In Europe, contact:
Hal Leonard Europe Limited
42 Wigmore Street
Marylebone, London, W1U 2RN
Email: info@halleonardeurope.com

In Australia, contact:
Hal Leonard Australia Pty. Ltd.
4 Lentara Court
Cheltenham, Victoria, 3192 Australia
Email: info@halleonard.com.au

FOREWORD

Glass Houses was released in 1980 and topped the Billboard charts for six weeks. It was the third album produced by Phil Ramone and featured Billy's first #1 single ("It's Still Rock and Roll to Me") along with three other top 40 hits ("You May Be Right," "Don't Ask Me Why," and "Sometimes a Fantasy"). It earned Billy a Grammy Award for "Best Male Rock Vocal Performance" and a Grammy nomination for "Album of the Year."

Following the success of *52nd Street* and several years of playing big arenas, Billy was feeling the need to write music with a bigger sound. He wanted to write harder edge songs with big guitars that would translate well in the larger venues he now performed in. The Yamaha CP80 Electric Grand became his piano of choice, giving a more aggressive and punchier sound to songs like "All for Leyna," "Sleeping with the Television On," and "I Don't Want to Be Alone".

Having played keyboards in Billy Joel's band since 1993, I have an inside perspective into his music. Accordingly, Billy asked that I review every note of the sheet music in his entire catalog of songs. As a pianist, he entrusted me with the task of correcting and re-transcribing each piece to ensure that the printed music represents each song exactly as it was written and recorded. This is the latest edition in our series of revised songbooks in the Billy Joel catalog.

The challenge with each folio in Billy's catalog is to find musical ways to combine his piano parts and vocal melodies into playable piano arrangements. First, the signature piano parts are transcribed and notated exactly as Billy played them. The vocal melodies are then transcribed and incorporated into the piano part in a way that preserves the original character of each song.

The instantly recognizable eighth-note piano chords in "All For Leyna" are played in many sections of the song. Although they may sound similar at first listen, the eighth-note piano chords in the intro and ending are different from each other and different from the way they are played in the choruses. I wrote these sections out rather than using repeats, so that Billy's

parts could be accurately notated as they appear in each section. In the verses, the piano part is combined with the bass and guitar parts creating a syncopation that supports the vocal melody and can all be played together. The double synth solo at the end of the song is not really possible to play on piano, so for this I created an amalgamation of the two parts (with some compromises) in order to make it playable with one hand and still sound like the record.

On "Don't Ask Me Why," the piano plays throughout the song and the vocal melody is easily playable on top of the chords. However, the solo section actually has *two* piano parts. The parts are very similar and are played in different octaves giving the solo a "four-hand" sound. For this section I created a single piano part that represents the basic sound of the two pianos, while the left hand plays the bass line.

The rocker "Close to the Borderline" is dominated by big guitars and doesn't have any piano on the record. For this one I created a piano part that plays the guitar riffs using heavier sounding voicings with lots of roots, fourths, and fifths to replicate the power chord sound of the big guitars. The same type of voicings are used for "Sometimes a Fantasy," and on this one I wrote out the dual lead guitar/synth part in the bridge and made it playable on piano.

"Through the Long Night" is a beautiful ballad characterized by the acoustic guitar and piano, which I combined into a single piano part that also includes the vocal melody.

All of the songs in this collection received the same astute attention to detail. The result is sheet music that is both accurate and enjoyable to play, and that remains true to the original performances.

Billy and I are pleased to present the revised and now accurate sheet music to the classic album *Glass Houses*.

Enjoy,

David Rosenthal
October 2019

CONTENTS

YOU MAY BE RIGHT

Words and Music by
BILLY JOEL

but you may __ be right. __

Well, _____ re-mem - ber how __ I found __
__ of all __ the years __
Instrumental

__ you there __ a - lone ___ in your __ e - lec - tric chair, __ I
__ you tried __ to find ___ some - one to sat - is - fy you

told you dirt - y jokes __ un - til you smiled. __
I might be __ as cra - zy as __ you say. __

SOMETIMES A FANTASY

Words and Music by
BILLY JOEL

16

DON'T ASK ME WHY

Words and Music by
BILLY JOEL

IT'S STILL ROCK AND ROLL TO ME

Words and Music by
BILLY JOEL

cheap pair of sneak - ers."   Next   phase,   new   wave,   dance craze;   an - y-ways, it's
whole lot - ta mon - ey." It's the next   phase,   new   wave,   dance craze;   an - y-ways, it's

still   rock and roll   to   me. _____
still   rock and roll   to   me. __

ALL FOR LEYNA

Words and Music by
BILLY JOEL

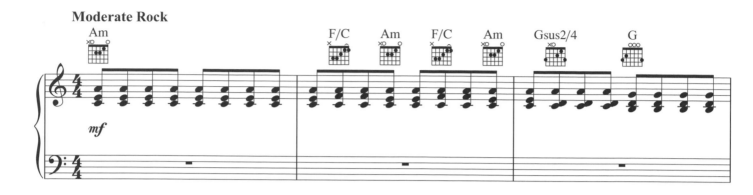

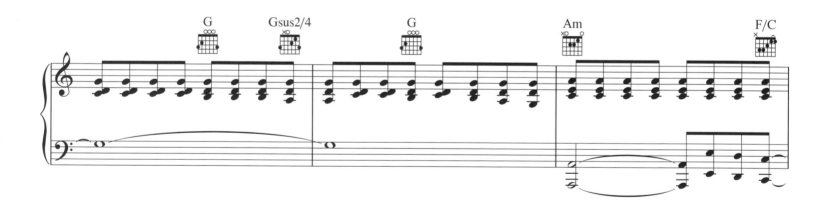

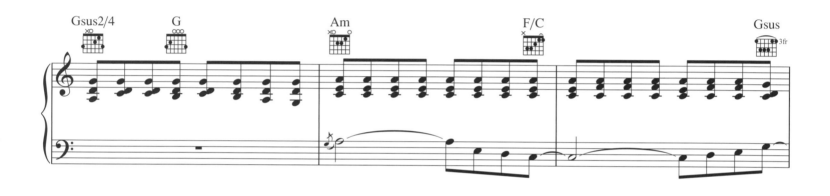

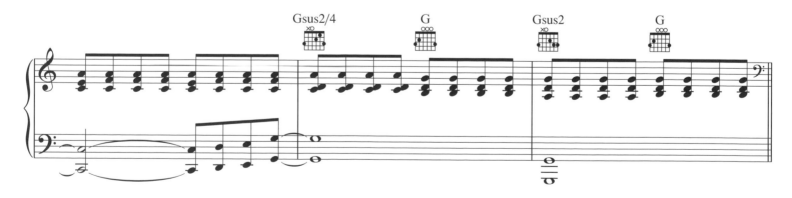

She   stood on the tracks,   wav - ing her arms   lead - ing me to
We   laid on the beach   watch - ing the tide.   She did - n't tell
Now   I'm in my room   watch - ing the tube,   tell - ing my - self

that third   rail   shock.   Quick as a wink   she changed her mind.
me there   were   rocks   un - der the waves   right off the shore.
she still   may   drop   o - ver to say   she's changed her mind.

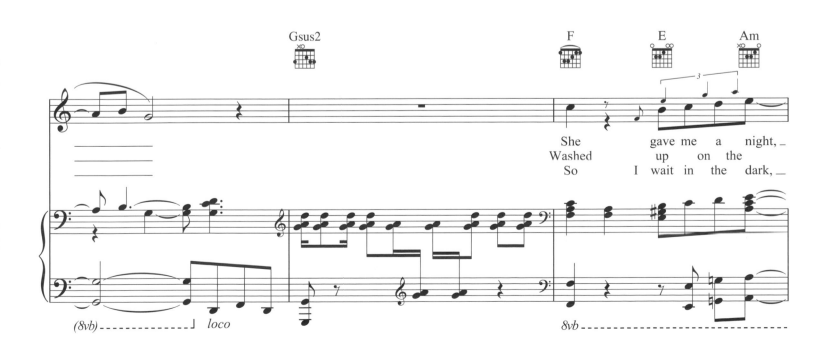

She   gave me a night,
Washed   up on the
So   I wait in the dark,

that's all it was.___ What will it take___ un - til___ I
sand bare - ly a - live,___ wish - ing the un - der - tow___ would
list - 'ning for her, 'stead of my old___ man say - ing,

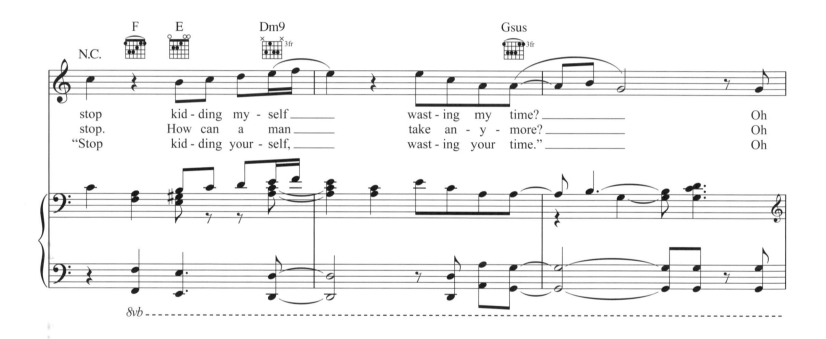

stop kid - ding my - self___ wast - ing my time?___ Oh
stop. How can a man___ take an - y - more?___ Oh
"Stop kid - ding your - self,___ wast - ing your time."___ Oh

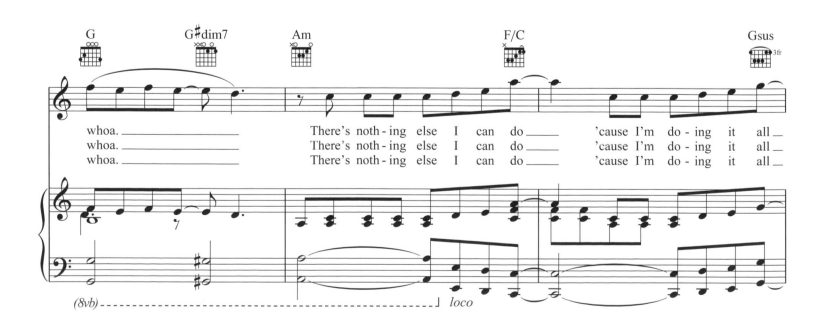

whoa.___ There's noth - ing else I can do___ 'cause I'm do - ing it all___
whoa.___ There's noth - ing else I can do___ 'cause I'm do - ing it all___
whoa.___ There's noth - ing else I can do___ 'cause I'm do - ing it all___

Repeat and Fade

All   for Ley - na.

I DON'T WANT TO BE ALONE

Words and Music by
BILLY JOEL

44

Repeat and Fade (vocal ad lib.)

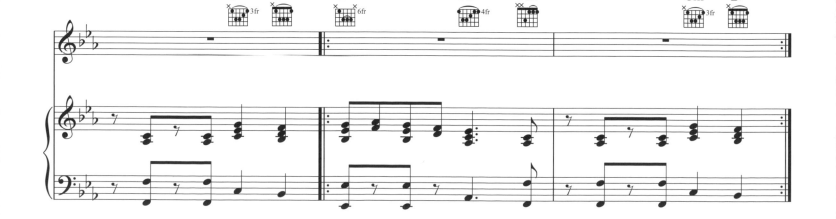

You May Be Right

Friday night I trashed your party
Saturday I said I'm sorry
Sunday came and trashed me out again
I was only having fun
Wasn't hurting anyone
And we all enjoyed the weekend for a change

I've been stranded in the combat zone
I walked through Bedford Stuy alone
→ Even rode my motorcycle in the rain
And you told me not to drive
But I made it home alive
So you said that only proves that I'm insane

You may be right / I may be crazy
→ But it just may be a lunatic you're looking for
Turn out the light / Don't try to save me
You may be wrong for all I know
→ but you may be right

Remember how I found you there
Alone in your electric chair
I told you dirty jokes until you smiled
You were lonely for a man
I said take me as I am
Cause you might enjoy some madness for a while

Sometimes A Fantasy

I didn't want to do it
But I got too lonely
I had to call you up
in the middle of the night
I know it's awful hard to try to make
Love long distance
But I really needed stimulation
Though it was only my imagination

chorus: It's just a fantasy
It's not the real thing
It's just a fantasy
It's not the real thing
Sometimes a fantasy
Is all you need

When am I gonna take control
Get ahold of my emotions
Why does it only seem to hit me
in the middle of the night
You told me there's a number
I can always dial for assistance
I don't want to deal with outside action
Only you can give me satisfaction

chorus:

Don't Ask Me Why

All the waiters in your grand café
Leave their tables when you blink
Every dog must have his everyday
Every drunk must have his drink
Don't wait for answers
Just take your chances
Don't ask me why

All your life you had to stand in line
Still you're standing on your feet
All your choices made you change your mind
Now your calendar's complete
Don't wait for answers
Just take your chances
Don't ask me why

You can say the human heart
Is only make - believe
And I am only fighting fire with fire
But you are still a victim of
The accidents you leave
As sure as I'm a victim of desire

All the servants in your new hotel
Throw their roses at your feet
Fool them all but baby I can tell
You're no stranger to the street
Don't ask for favors
Don't talk to strangers
Don't ask me why

Yesterday you were an only child
Now your ghosts have gone away
You Can You can kill them in the classic style
Now you parlez vous - Francais
Don't look for answers
You took your chances
Don't ask me why

Yesterday you were an only child
Now your ghosts have gone away
You can kill them in the classic style
Now you parlez vous Francais
Don't look for answers
You took your chances
Don't ask me why

SLEEPING WITH THE TELEVISION ON

Words and Music by
BILLY JOEL

gun in ___ your hand until you're point-ing it and stun-ning their sens - es. All ___
kind of chanc - es, dear, to-mor-row morn-ing you'll wake up with the white _ noise. All ___

___ night long, all ___ night long. You'll shoot 'em down be-cause you're
___ night long, all ___ night long. You're on - ly stand-ing there 'cause

All ___ night long, all ___ night long.

wait-ing for some - bod - y good ___ to come on. ___ But you'll be
some-bod - y once ___ did some - bod - y wrong. ___ But you'll be

to me. Your eyes are say-ing talk to me. Talk ___ to me.

But you won't hear a word, 'cause it just ___

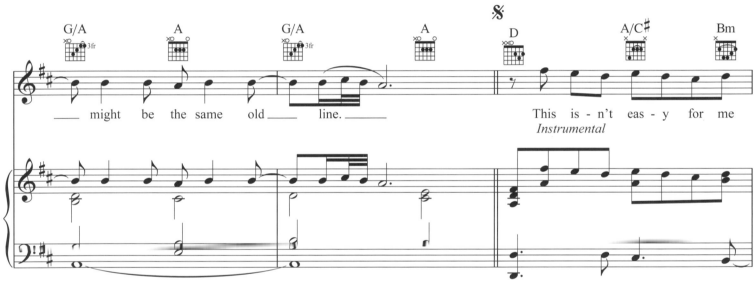

___ might be the same old ___ line. ___ This is-n't eas-y for me

Instrumental

to say, Di-ane. I know you don't need an-y-bod-y's pro-tec - tion. ___

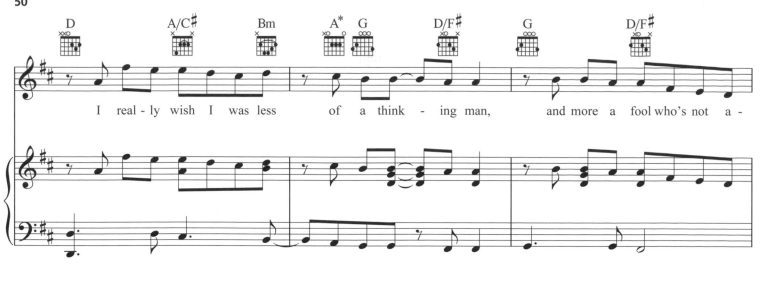

I real-ly wish I was less of a think - ing man, and more a fool who's not a-

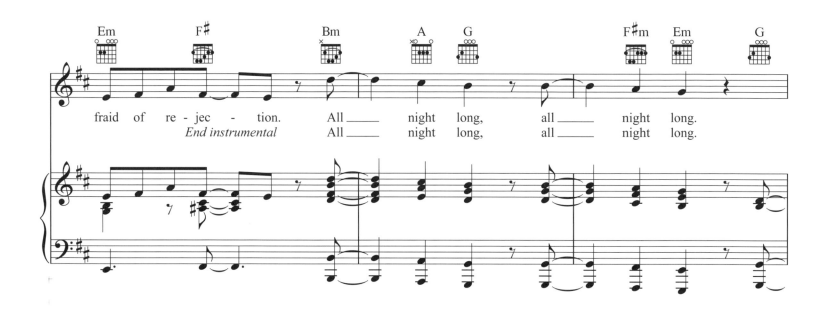

fraid of re - jec - tion. All ___ night long, all ___ night long.

End instrumental All ___ night long, all ___ night long.

Oh, _____ all ___ night long, all _

I'll just be stand-ing here 'cause I know I don't __ have the guts ___ to come on. ___

We'll just be stand-ing here 'cause some-bod - y might __ do some - bod - y wrong. ___

*Omit A chord 2nd time.

LEYNA

She stood on the tracks
Waving her arms, leading me to that
Third rail = shock - quick as a wink
She changed her mind....

She gave me a night
That's all it was
What will it take until I stop
Kidding myself, wasting my time

chorus: Nothing else I can do
cause I'm doing it all for Leyna
Don't want anyone new
cause I'm living it all for Leyna
Nothing in it for you
cause I'm giving it all to Leyna

We laid on the beach
~~watching the tide~~, wishing ~~the undertow~~
~~would~~ stop, ~~how can a man take anymore~~
watching the tide, she didn't kill me
There were rocks under the waves
right off the shore

---

wasted up on the sand, barely alive
wishing the undertow would stop
How can a man take anymore

chorus: ⌇ _____

I'm failing in school
Losing my friends
Making my family lose their minds
I don't want to eat
I don't want to sleep
I only want Leyna one more time

Now I'm in my room
watching the tube
Telling myself she still may drop
over to say - she's changed her mind
So, I wait in the dark
Listening for her, instead of my old man
saying stop... kidding yourself, wasting your time

chorus: ⌇ _____

Sleeping With The Television ON

I've been watching you waltz all night Diane
slowly going a way behind your defenses
They never notice the zap gun in your hand
Until you're pointing it and stunning their senses

All night long, All night long
You'll shoot 'em down because you're waiting
for somebody good to come on
But you'll be sleeping with the television on

You say you're looking for someone solid here
You can't be bothered with those
'just for the night boys'
Tonight unless you take some kind of chances dear
Tomorrow morning you'll wake up with the white noise

All night long, All night long
You're only standing there
Cause somebody once did somebody wrong
But you'll be sleeping with the television on

Your eyes are saying
Talk to me, talk to me
But your attitude is 'Don't waste my time'
But you won't hear a word
Cause it just might be the same old line

This isn't easy for me to say Diane
I know you don't need anybody's protection
I really wish I was less of a thinking man
and more a fool who's not afraid of rejection

All night long, All night long
I'll just be standing here
'Cause I know I don't have
the guts to come on
And I'll be sleeping with the television on

Your eyes are saying
Talk to me, talk to me
But my attitude is
"Boy, don't waste your time"
But I won't say a word
'Cause it just might be
somebody else's same old line

C'ETAIT TOI
(You Were the One)

Words and Music by
BILLY JOEL

Moderately

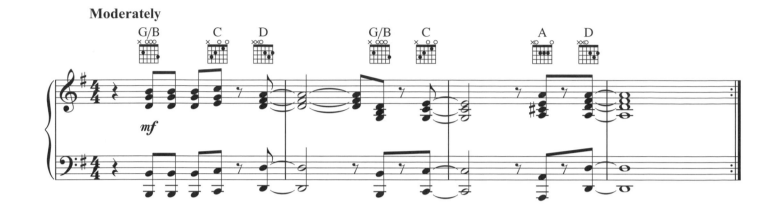

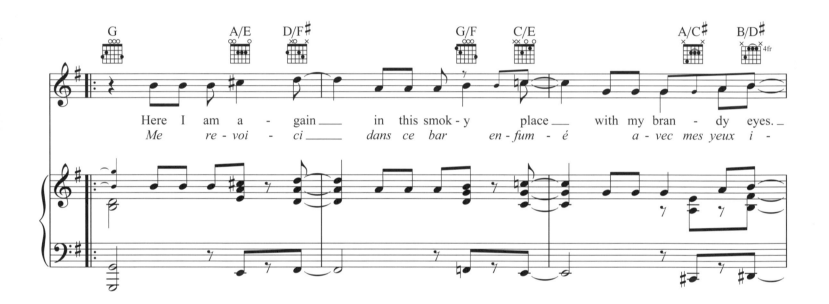

Here I am a - gain___ in this smok - y place___ with my bran - dy eyes.___
Me re - voi - ci___ dans ce bar en - fum - é a - vec mes yeux i -

___ *vres*   I'm talk - ing to___ my - self:___ you were the one,___
Je me parle___ à___ moi même.___ Ooh,___ c'é - tait toi,___

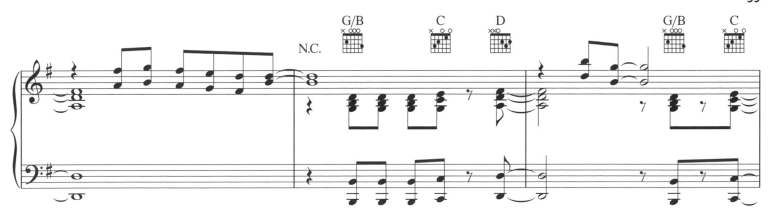

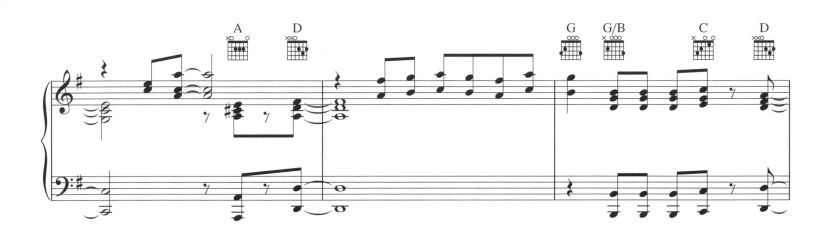

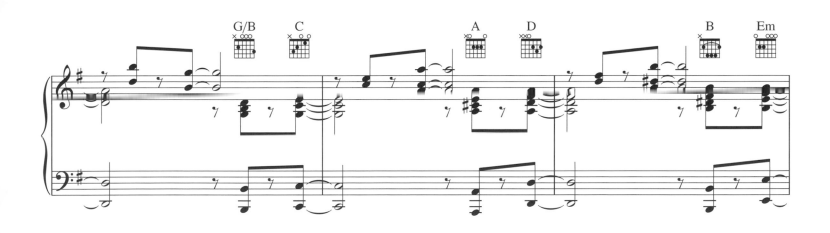

Repeat and Fade

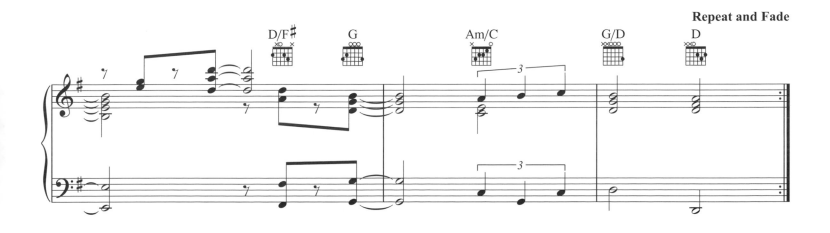

CLOSE TO THE BORDERLINE

Words and Music by
BILLY JOEL

To Coda ⊕

ledge looks like an-oth-er su - i - cide.___ She wants to
ei - ther way, A - mer - i - can shoved in - to the lost and found.___ The

hit those bricks 'cause the news___ at six got - ta stick to a dead - line.
no nukes yell we're gon - na all___ go to hell with the next big melt - down.

While the mil - lion-aires hide in Beek - man Place, the
I got re - mote con - trol and a col - or T. V., I

bag lad - ies throw their bones___ in my face. I get at - tacked by a kid with
don't change chan - nels so they must change me. I got real close friends that are

64

THROUGH THE LONG NIGHT

Words and Music by
BILLY JOEL

Moderately slow

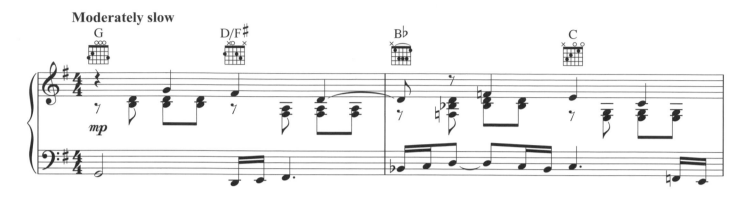

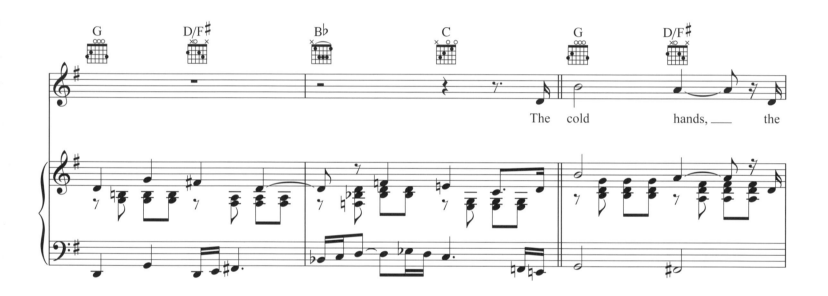

The cold hands, ___ the

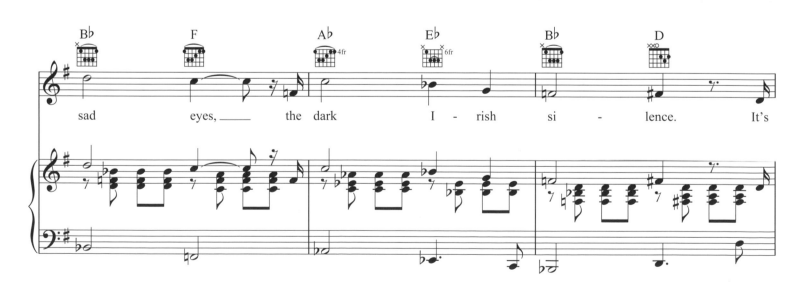

sad eyes, ___ the dark I - rish si - lence. It's